LANDING LIGHT

Also by Don Paterson

POETRY

Nil Nil

God's Gift to Women

The Eyes

The White Lie: New and Selected Poetry

EDITOR

101 Sonnets

Robert Burns: Selected Poems

Last Words (with Jo Shapcott)

Don't Ask Me What I Mean (with Clare Brown)

New British Poetry (with Charles Simic)

The Book of Shadows (Aphorisms)

LANDING LIGHT

Poems

Don Paterson

Graywolf Press
SAINT PAUL, MINNESOTA

Publication of this volume is made possible in part by a grant provided by the Minnesota State Arts Board, through an appropriation by the Minnesota State Legislature; a grant from the Wells Fargo Foundation Minnesota; and a grant from the National Endowment for the Arts, which believes that a great nation deserves great art. Significant support has also been provided by the Bush Foundation; Target and Mervyn's with support from the Target Foundation; the McKnight Foundation; and other generous contributions from foundations, corporations, and individuals. To these organizations and individuals we offer our heartfelt thanks.

First published in 2003 by Faber and Faber Limited, London

Published by Graywolf Press
2402 University Avenue, Suite 203
Saint Paul, Minnesota 55114
All rights reserved.

www.graywolfpress.org

Published in the United States of America

ISBN 1-55597-417-1

2 4 6 8 9 7 5 3 1

First Graywolf Printing, 2005

Library of Congress Control Number: 2004109267

Cover design: Christa Schoenbrodt, Studio Haus

Cover photograph: Rubberball Productions

for J.C.Z. and R.T.Z.

Contents

Acknowledgments

Acknowledgments are due to the following: BBC Radio Four, BBC Radio Three, Dundee Contemporary Arts, *Flora Poetica, The Gift, Landfall, London Review of Books, Near East Review, New Republic, Poem for the Day, Poetry Review,* The Poetry Society, *Prime, Verse.*

The author would like to express his gratitude to the Scottish Arts Council and to the Society of Authors for their support.

LANDING LIGHT

Luing

When the day comes, as the day surely must,
when it is asked of you, and you refuse
to take that lover's wound again, that cup
of emptiness that is our one completion,

I'd say go here, maybe, to our unsung
innermost isle: Kilda's antithesis,
yet still with its own tiny stubborn anthem,
its yellow milkwort and its stunted kye.

Leaving the motherland by a two-car raft,
the littlest of the fleet, you cross the minch
to find yourself, if anything, now deeper
in her arms than ever – sharing her breath,

watching the red vans sliding silently
between her hills. In such intimate exile,
who'd believe the burn behind the house
the straitened ocean written on the map?

Here, beside the fordable Atlantic,
reborn into a secret candidacy,
the fontanelles reopen one by one
in the palms, then the breastbone and the brow,

aching at the shearwater's wail, the rowan
that falls beyond all seasons. One morning
you hover on the threshold, knowing for certain
the first touch of the light will finish you.

St Brides: Sea-Mail

Now they have gone
we are sunk, believe me.
Their scentless oil, so volatile
it only took one stray breath on its skin
to set it up – it was our sole
export, our currency
and catholicon.

There was a gland
below each wing, a duct
four inches or so down the throat;
though it was tiresome milking them by hand
given the rumour of their infinite
supply, and the blunt fact
of our demand.

After the cull
we'd save the carcasses,
bind the feet and fan the wings,
sew their lips up, empty out their skulls
and carry them away to hang
in one of the drying-houses,
twelve to a pole.

By Michaelmas
they'd be so light and stiff
you could lift one up by its ankle
or snap the feathers from its back like glass.
Where their eyes had been were inkwells.
We took them to the cliffs
and made our choice.

Launching them,
the trick was to 'make
a little angel': ring- and fore-
fingers tucked away, pinkie and thumb
spread wide for balance, your
middle finger hooked
under the sternum.

Our sporting myths:
the windless, perfect day
McNicol threw beyond the stac;
how, ten years on, MacFarlane met his death
to a loopback. Whatever our luck,
by sunset, they'd fill the bay
like burnt moths.

The last morning
we shuffled out for parliament
their rock was empty, and the sky clear
of every wren and fulmar and whitewing.
The wind has been so weak all year
I post this more in testament
than hope or warning.

Sliding on Loch Ogil

Remember, brother soul, that day spent cleaving
nothing from nothing, like a thrown knife?
Then there was no arriving and no leaving,
just a dream of the disintricated life –
crucified and free, the still man moving,
the balancing his work, the wind his wife.

Waking with Russell

Whatever the difference is, it all began
the day we woke up face-to-face like lovers
and his four-day-old smile dawned on him again,
possessed him, till it would not fall or waver;
and I pitched back not my old hard-pressed grin
but his own smile, or one I'd rediscovered.
Dear son, I was *mezzo del cammin*
and the true path was as lost to me as ever
when you cut in front and lit it as you ran.
See how the true gift never leaves the giver:
returned and redelivered, it rolled on
until the smile poured through us like a river.
How fine, I thought, this waking amongst men!
I kissed your mouth and pledged myself forever.

The Thread

Jamie made his landing in the world
so hard he ploughed straight back into the earth.
They caught him by the thread of his one breath
and pulled him up. They don't know how it held.
And so today I thank what higher will
brought us to here, to you and me and Russ,
the great twin-engined swaying wingspan of us
roaring down the back of Kirrie Hill

and your two-year-old lungs somehow out-revving
every engine in the universe.
All that trouble just to turn up dead
was all I thought that long week. Now the thread
is holding all of us: look at our tiny house,
son, the white dot of your mother waving.

Incunabula

Who are these tonsured scribes at facing desks?
Sunk in their slow proofreading, thumbs
locked in their mouths as they roll between them
the globe of water in whose seagreen disk
they magnify the dreadful minuscule –
knowing how little will make the difference,
that a single letter lost or doubled ruins
not just the manuscript but the whole school?

America

All afternoon we stood watch on the wharf
for what might now be summoned and evicted
till one wave slowly turned and curled and sickened
and boked up a man. He hung there for a second
and somewhere in that second was perfected
then came apart and fell into the surf.

The Forest of the Suicides

Inferno, Canto xiii

Who are these pietàs?
The shadows of ringdoves chanting, but easing nothing.

Sylvia Plath, *Winter Trees*

Nessus was still midriver, trotting back
to the far bank, when suddenly I found
I was back in a dark wood, this time unmarked
by any path at all. I looked around.

Each barren, blood-black tree was like a plate
from a sailor's book of knots, its branches bent
and pleached and coiled as if to demonstrate
some novel and ingenious kind of torment.

In the topmost branches of those wretched trees
I saw the Snatcher build its nest; whose kin
drove Aeneas from the Strophades,
spoiled his table, and spat out his ruin.

There it squats, its human face all wrong
above its fledged gut, wide-winged, razor-clawed.
With its avian knack of mimicry, its song
is a loop-tape of the children it has tortured.

I felt so desolate, it gave me a start
to hear his voice. 'Now, friend; before we leave
stand still for just a moment, and listen hard.
This place is almost too strange to believe.'

Below the pitiful sobs and chokes and cries
lower moans were echoing through the glade,
yet I saw no one to make them. 'Master, why
do they hide from us?' I asked. 'Are they afraid?'

Then he replied: 'Break off a little spray
from any plant here: then I guarantee
things will become clearer.' I snapped away
a twig from the bush that stood closest to me.

In the trunk, a red mouth opened like a cut.
Then a voice screamed out 'Why are you tearing me?'
It was a woman's voice. Blood began to spurt
from the broken tip. 'You, are you hearing me?

When exactly did I earn *your* scorn?
Supposing I'd a heart black as a snake's,
I was a woman once, that now am thorn.
What would a little pity have set you back?'

Just in the way a split cord of green wood,
lit at one end, starts to spit and blister
at the other, so it was the words and blood
bubbled from her splintered mouth. 'Dear sister,'

my guide interrupted, 'if only my poor friend
had recalled what I had written of this hell
I know he never would have raised his hand
against you; but the truth is so incredible

I urged him on. Forgive his ignorance –
but he can make amends; just tell him who
you were, and how you came here. When he returns
to the upper world, your fame can bloom anew.'

And then the tree laughed. 'Bravo sir! Well said.
You'd spend a lifetime trying to put it worse.
In my design, that scalded beach ahead
would be reserved for the biographers.

And if it's self-improvement your friend seeks
perhaps it's courtesy you need to teach . . .
Ah. But you can see that I am weak,
and lured into a little human speech.

Very well. When I was small, I held both keys
that fitted my father's heart; which I unlocked
and locked again with such a delicate ease
he felt no turning, and he heard no click.

He desired no other confidence but mine;
nor would I permit one. I was so bound
to my splendid office that, when he resigned,
I followed. They had to dig me from the ground.

So the post remained, and I remained as true;
and, in time, I came to interview
for his successor. None of them would do
until a black shape cut the light in two

and at once I knew my ideal candidate.
But that green-eyed courtesan, that vice of courts
who had always stalked his halls and kept his gate –
the years had steeped me in her sullen arts

and my tongue grew hot with her abysmal need.
Slowly, I turned it on my second Caesar
until it seemed to him his every deed
did nothing but disgrace his predecessor.

So he left me too; but the tongue still burned away
till I sung the bright world only to estrange it,
and prophesied my end so nakedly
mere decency insisted I arrange it.

My mind, then, in its voice of reasoned harm
told me Death would broker my release
from every shame, and back into his arms;
so I made my date. It was bad advice.

But if your friend should somehow cut a path
back to the light, then tell them I betrayed
the spirit, not the letter of the oath –
by far the lesser crime in our dark trade.'

My master hissed: 'Listen – she's silent now.
Quickly, don't just throw away your chance;
ask her, if there's more you wish to know.'
I replied: 'My lord, you know the questions

I brought with me; so ask what I would ask.
I have no stomach for this conversation.'
He nodded. 'That this man may fulfil his task
and witness for you at his final station,

imprisoned soul – if you could bear to – say
just how the spirit comes to be so caught
in these terrible spasms, and if perhaps one day
it might be wrested free of its own knots.'

Long seconds passed before she spoke again.
'Remember: though these words are some relief,
the breath I draw to fill them gives a pain
beyond your knowledge. I will be brief.

The very instant that the furious soul
tears itself from the flesh, some inverse power
bundles it screaming down the sudden hole
that opens in the bed or bath or floor;

then Minos directs it to the seventh pit
where it spins down to this starless nursery
to seed wherever fortune tosses it.
There it roots, and drives up through the clay

to grow into the shape of its own anguish.
Finally, the Harpies swarm to crop
the leaves and buds – a blessing and a scourge,
since it pains us, and yet lets the pain escape.

And like you, at the final clarion,
we'll return to fish our bodies from the ground,
but never again to wear them: such is the sin
of our ingratitude. Instead, we'll drag them down

to this dark street; and here they'll stay, strung out
forever in their miserable parade –
naked and still, each hung like a white coat
on the hook of its own alienated shade.'

The Hunt

By the time he met his death
I'd counted off twelve years
and in the crossed and harrowed path
could read my whole career

the nights of circling alone
in corridors of earth
the days like paler nights, my lodestone
dying to the north

while I lived by what uncertain meat
was left from his repast
and what rainwater and bitter light
could worm in through the crust

And in that time my axe had swung
no closer to his neck
than the echo of his sullen tongue
or the hot smell of his wake

Though now and then I'd find a scrap
of gold thread in the dirt
and once, a corner of the map
she'd sewn into my shirt

I had no use for either here
being so long deranged
by the tortuous familiar
as once I'd been the strange

Then one day near the heart, making
a break in my patrol
I drained my flask and leant my aching
back against the wall

Across the way I saw a gap.
I conjured up a flame
and cupped it down twelve narrow steps
into an airless tomb

I gave the light from side to side.
The little vault unfurled
its mockery of the life I'd led
back in the upper world

The walls were lined with skinbound books
the floor with braided hair
in the corner, stuck with shite and wax
a bone table, a bone chair

On the table lay a dish of gall
and by it, for my lamp
a thighbone propping up a skull
inside, a tallow stump

I gently slid my spill into
one eye, then cut my breath
until a thin partitioned glow
strained out between the teeth

It was then my misbegotten quarry
swam up from the gloom
loitering in the darker doorway
to a second room

We shuffled close, like two old fools
and stood there for an age
trying to recollect the rules
by which we were engaged

I read no terror in his frown
no threat and no intrigue
the massive head was canted down
in pity or fatigue

so I put my hand out, hoping this
might break our dead impasse
and he had made to tender his
when my hand hit the glass

Letter to the Twins

. . . for it is said, they went to school at Gabii, and were well
instructed in letters, and other accomplishments befitting their birth.
And they were called Romulus and Remus (from *ruma*, the dug), as
we had before, because they were found sucking the wolf.

Plutarch, *Parallel Lives*

Dear sons – for I am not, as you believed,
your uncle – forgive me now my dereliction.
In those nine months the single thought that grieved
me most was not your terrible instruction

in the works of men, the disillusionments –
Nanking and Srebrenica, Babi Yar –
you, bent above those tables of events
by whose low indices you might infer

how far you'd fallen. No, it was instead
the years you'd spend reconstituting all
the billion tedious skills of humanhood:
the infinite laws of Rome, the protocols

of every minor court and consulate –
that city that must rise up from its razed
foundations, mirrored and immaculate,
for as often as we come back to this place.

In sum, they might account it a disaster
but whatever I did, I did it as a deft
composer of the elements, the master
of all terrestrial drag and spin and heft;

look at this hand – the way it knows how light
to grip the pen, how far above the brim
to fill the cup, or hard to steer the kite,
or slowly it can travel through the flame.

More, it knows the vanity of each.
But were I to commend just one reserve
of study – one I promise that will teach
you nothing of *use,* and so not merely serve

to deepen your attachment or your debt,
where each small talent added to the horde
is doubled in its spending, and somehow yet
no more or less than its own clean reward –

it would be this: the honouring of your lover.
Learn this and she will guide you, if not home
then at least to its true memory. Then wherever
the world loses you, in her you are the same.

First, she will address you in a tongue
so secret she must close her mouth on yours.
In the curves and corners of this silent song
will lie the whole code of your intercourse.

Then, as you break, at once you understand
how the roses of her breast will draw in tight
at your touch, how that parched scrubland
between her thighs breaks open into wet

suddenly, as though you'd found the stream
running through it like a seam of milk;
know, by its tiny pulse and its low gleam
just where the pearl sits knuckled in its silk,

how that ochre-pink anemone relaxes
and unknots under your light hand and white spit;
and how that lovely mouth that has no kiss
will take the deepest you can plant in it;

and how to make that shape that boys, alas,
will know already as the sign for *gun*
yet slide it with a woman's gentleness
till you meet that other muzzle coming down.

Now, in all humility, retrace
your steps, that you might understand in full
the privilege that brought you to this place,
that let you know the break below the wool:

and as you lie there by her side, and feel
the wet snout of her womb nuzzle and lather
your fingertips – then you might recall
your mother; or her who said she was your mother.

A Fraud

I was twenty, and crossing
a field near Bridgefoot
when I saw something glossing
the toe of my boot

and bent down to spread
the bracken and dock
where a tiny wellhead
had broken the rock

It strained through the gap
as a little clear tongue
that replenished its shape
by the shape of its song

Then it spoke. It said *Son*
I've no business with you.
Whatever I own
is the next fellow's due.

But if I'm his doom
or Castalian spring –
your directive's the same:
keep walking.

But before it could soak
back into the stone
I dropped like a hawk
and I made it my own

and I bit its slim root
until it confessed
then swallowed its shout
in the cave of my breast

Now two strangers shiver
under one roof
the one who delivers
the promise and proof

and the one I deploy
for the poem or the kiss.
It gives me no joy
to tell you this.

The Reading

The first time I came to your wandering attention
my name was Simonides. Poets,
whose air of ingratitude forms in the womb,
have reason at least to thank me:
I invented the thing you now call the commission.
Oh – and one other frivolity
refined by Aquinas, tuned up by Bruno
and perfected by Hannibal Lecter.

All in good time. But first to the theme
of this evening's address: the reading.
It was not a good poem, if I say so myself.
As good as the fee, though, and better
than him who that day bought my praises: a man
of so little virtue to sing of
I ended up fleshing it out, as you do,
with something I'd found in the drawer –

a hymn that I'd made a while back, for the twin sons
of Leda, the Dioscuri.
At the feast he had held in his own dubious honour
the little king signed me to start;
but though they were quiet for my halfbaked encomium –
applauding like seals when I'd finished –
his guests, when I started to read from my own stuff,
returned to their wolfing and hollering.

The king, though, was silent. My lyric economies
had not, so it seemed, gone unnoticed.
When he offered me only one-half the struck price,
I made too much show of my anger
knowing, I dare say, his wrath the more just –
but right then I seemed to go deaf;
every eye turned on me, narrowed – at which point
I thought it a smart move to drop it.

However, I fixed each man's face in my mind,
each man at his rank at the table
(that trick of mine; your coupons, O my rapt listeners,
I'll have nailed by the end of this poem).
Then this. A young slave-girl ran into the hall
then right up to me, with this message:
two golden-haired boys had arrived at the gate,
and wanted to talk with me. Urgently.

I asked that I might be excused, a small boon
they were more than delighted to grant,
and took a slow stroll to the gate. I found no one.
Bloody kids. I turned back to the hall
and cursed them to heaven. Heaven replied
without hesitation or stint: a great thunderbolt
aimed not at me, but the ridgepole.
The roof groaned and splintered, sagged for a moment
then cracked, and came down on the lot of them.

After the dust and the sirens had died
the wives all came wailing and weeping
to claim what they could of their tenderised menfolk.
Alas, they were all so disfigured
no one could work out whose husband was whose.
Of course I could. *The redbeard? Just there,*
by the fire. And the scarface? The door. And the hawknose?
Poor woman: look under your feet.

I picked my way down to head of the table
and held the fixed gaze of my patron
as I knelt in the rafters and carefully counted
the rest of my fee from his purse.

A Talking Book

Welcome children! First, to those rare birds
for whom all journeyings are heavenwards,
who always wing it, mapless and alone;
to those undecided shades in Waterstones,
trapped between the promise and the cost;
to Umso Cairns, whose number has been lost;
to those precisians on the proper route,
who have diligently ploughed this far on foot
by way of bastard title, biog note
acknowledgements and prefatory quote;
to those kabbalists and chrysometronomes
who drag each sentence through their fine-toothed combs,
all set to prove the Great Beast lies at slumber
in the ISBN or the barcode number;
and a big hi! to those holders, old and new
of the critic's one-day travel-pass (I too
have known that sudden quickening of the pulse
when something looks a bit like something else;
but if all you ever listen to is Hindemith
the very larksong seems to give you wind of it –
thus those lads so especially attuned
should first look to the wee melodeon
of their own hearts. But those Boeotians
who like to shove their poems into tins
marked either *ah!* or *hahaha!* or *hmm* . . .
might now be best advised to leave the room).
To the academy's swift and unannounced inspection:
this page knows nothing of its self-reflexion,
its author-death, or its *mise-en-abîme*.
Relax! Things are exactly as they seem.

The charge of being clever, coy or cute
I will not even bother to refute,
there being no I to speak of. Look around
the plane or lift or john or underground:
you are alone. Now think upon that net
of happenstance, velleity and fate
that catches us together in this way:
the near-miraculous singularity
of the present moment. Okay: now let's
say you're in the bath, lathering your pits
with – your Pears impractically thin –
a horrible red lump of glycerine
in which a tiny plastic replica
of Gromit is embedded, his snout and paw
freed on the humanitarian whim
of a girl you know who just can't help but sym-
pathise with everything. The soap sticks
in your oxterhair; an ill-advised dub mix
of *Song Composed in August* farts away
on the wee radio downstairs, while you essay,
with your free hand, to hold this page aloft.
A marker might be placed here, in the daft
book of your life – a wild cry from the street,
say; except it won't. So what we get
is an instance neither shameful nor exemplary,
just the only one. Forgive my wild extempore:
this poem's initial purpose is to stress
the specificity of its address.
To that board in 30–75 AD
who sit in judgement over what, today,

29

will be preserved or cast to the abyss
I speak not your Highnesses *en masse*
but to Zarkon up from Mare Imbrium
whose purple drink is coming back on him.

Though God forbid that I propose to you
you're anywhere but right here – halfway through
this dark tale of the author's final fight
for that perpetually vacant belt of light
in the high ring of the sunscorched upper ether –
that young man's sport – before he falls, unfeathered
and half-blind back to middle earth to stand
alone in the assuaging shadowlands
and seek the means by which he might appraise
that lenient and sweetening compromise
between the vision and his earthly term,
the happy marriage of the rose and worm.

Oh no. Be sure this song is just for you.
It will, no doubt, be wasted on a few –
unmoved by the recto or the verso,
they stand before Apollo's ancient torso
and all it says is *You must lose some weight.*
Let's not count you among their number. Right:
now we're of one mind now, i.e. yours –
a little psychometric test. Now choose
from the following (you have my word this won't
go any further than ourselves). The present
is the wall of glass on which you rest your brow
while wailing inwardly the one word *now*;

the present is the wall between two rooms
through which you push the ghosts you reassume
half-seconds later; the present is the wall,
this side of which you rigorously patrol,
between something and nothing; it leaks.
The present is the wall that brick by brick
builds itself before you, while you haul
yourself upward, then lose your grip and fall.
The present is the wall of sea thrown up
by some one-in-a-billion ontic burp,
a standing wave that has no beach to hit;
or the present is the wall on which you sit
watching your hands get old. (Look down there now:
O fellow matter, do you remember how
they were once so small and round and free from blame?
How ever did you stop grieving for them?)

If you answered a) b) c) d) e) or f)
you're not taking this seriously enough.

For at the bottom of this escalator
you are nearly two-thirds down, a cloven altar
awaits your sacrifice or desecration.
Now shake yourself awake, and please stay patient.
Shortly you will stand before it, torn
between the gates of ivory and horn,
the left, the right, the road that gets you lost
and the one boldly eschewed by Robert Frost,
Scheherazade's forever and a night
or the numbered days of Sodom; black or white,

shit creek or happy valley, scent or stink,
the tower or pit, the palace or the sink –
till you bow to that infernal contradiction
here, in the dead heart of serious fiction.

By all means, turn the page or close the book.
But first, imagine how this world would look
were it not duly filtered, cropped and strained
into that pinhole camera you call a brain
by whose inverted dim imaginings
you presume to question it. So many things
are hidden from you. Luckily. Here's one.

There are two earths, and for each earth a sun.
The lower of them lights the world that swills
as heavily within this torpid circle
as ours does in its brandyglass of weather.
You never meet your underself, other
than in dreams or sickness; but maybe once
a year, some prodigy of circumstance
sees the two lock on a common feature –
a book, a bed, a wall – and then the nature
of their crossing is revealed.
                                    It is always
dusk at the crossing, whatever your watch says.
What you see here is the world of men-as-mass.
The army of the underfolk will pass
quite unaware of you, stood half-transparent
in the muddle of your sub-enlightenment.
One stops in his slow march to make his sperm
and smear it on the ancient porphyry herm

on which another might then gently lower
herself, and then rejoin the silent river.
Such is your human love.
                                Anyway this is one
such uniquity. This book you hold
is even sadder in the other world.
Let me introduce you to you. No:
my pleasure. Yes, it's dark. Not far to go.
As ever in these straits, you have three choices:
stay here at the crossing with the crosses,
and live whatever kind of grim shelf-life
you live, hung on the high crux of yourself;
or carefully unroll the palliasse
on which your mind was borne into this place,
shut or mark or bin or burn this book,
then lie back and forget we ever spoke.

Or this. That wall we spoke of earlier,
the chains of now, the tyranny of here
(stay with me, though the bed is cool and soft)
– remember? Here is the secret long vouchsafed
to the brotherhood of things and things alone.

The present is a trick played in your head.
You already walk among the mineral dead.
You have slipped off into time the way a leaf
will wither and detach itself and drift
into a stream, not knowing its free spirit
is death, its animation lent to it.
There is no wall. Pick up your bed. Walk through it.
Last chance, friend. So do it or don't do it.

The Rat

A young man wrote a poem about a rat.
It was the best poem ever written about a rat.
To read it was to ask the rat to perch
on the arm of your chair until you turned the page.
So we wrote to him, but heard nothing; we called,
and called again; then finally we sailed
to the island where he kept the only shop
and rapped his door until he opened up.

We took away his poems. Our hands shook
with excitement. We read them on lightboxes,
under great lamps. They were not much good.
So then we offered what advice we could
on his tropes and turns, his metrical comportment,
on the wedding of the word to the event,
and suggested that he might read this or that.
We said *Now: write us more poems like The Rat.*

All we got was cheek from him. Then silence.
We gave up on him. Him with his green arrogance
and ingratitude and his one lucky strike.
But today I read The Rat again. Its reek
announced it; then I saw its pisshole stare;
line by line it strained into the air.
Then it hissed. *For all the craft and clever-clever
you did not write me, fool. Nor will you ever.*

Form

Thon March forenoon
I jinked the grieve
and lowped the yett
to Airlie's grove
and in a pit
in Airlie's weir
fund the roots
o a deid sauch
happed in ice,
an strippit awa
the burnin case –
a bricht claa
a pure sang
o sauch-roots,
I mind I thocht
if this wis aa
there wis til it:
dook the thing
in the winterburn
then pu' the sark
o broad daylicht
fae its back
and raise it
to the cauld sun –
shocked
commemorit

jinked – dodged; *grieve* – farm-bailiff; *lowped* – jumped; *yett* – gate;
sauch – willow; *happed* – bound; *claa* – claw; *dook* – plunge; *sark* –
shirt

The Box

If it can stay
at its post,
cross-braced
between
the world
and the
weather
this one
will see
me out:
behold
its dark
scoured
innards,
fragrant
with tea
and rust,
its drum-tight
blown-egg feel, the cone
of air before it, wired and tense
as a lover by a telephone. Bert
Kwakkel,   my Dutch
luthier,   emptied
so much wood out of the wood
it takes no more than a dropped shoe
or a cleared throat on the hall landing
to set its little blue moan off again.
I port it to its stand. I let it
still. I contemplate it
like a skull.

The Last Waltz

for T.G., again

I am, demonstrably I guess, in heaven:
on the wing again, the bellied engine
of our split-new SilkAir 777

drawing our unwavering beeline
for Blighty; above it all, the seablue sky,
its little ghost-Dunkirk. And I feel fine –

in one white fist, a half of cooking whisky,
in the other, a photocopy of that icon
of Padmasambhava known as *Looks Like Me*

while my guitars let out a long, detuned yawn
in the dark hold, knowing I will torture them
no longer. Now the sun is going down

and staying down this time. We're nearly home.
I watch the condensation gently throb
across the window like a fleet of sperm.

At least the last job felt like the last job;
this morning, thirty hours ago, we'd sat
like geckos underneath the sky's great slab

in our seventh day of Sarawak's bone-heat
no-weather, inhaling through our teeth
and toying with our Weetabix and jackfruit.

Silence. *Turned out nice again.* Slow breath.
Away and fuck off. Silence. There is no bomb
like the jungle-bomb, the rain-forest death:

long will I recall that infrasonic boom,
that verdant hush that spread like a bad word
around the final error in our program –

the Iban folk-song that we'd been assured
was their rallying, their *I Belong To Glasgow,*
their *Cwm Rhhonda.* What people had been stirred

by its drab burden we may never know
but can rule one out with utter certainty.
The last note sang into the heart of Borneo;

a lonely breadfruit thumped out of a tree;
one rabid monkey howled twelve miles upriver.
You manfully squared up to the PA

and with a Englishness that made me shiver
informed the nation you would get your coat.
This time we knew the truth of it: whatever

our visas might have said, we'd undershot
the mark. I knew the shame the letter feels
when it makes its address but its stamps fall short.

Last night, half-garrotted in the coils
of my obscure native bedding, completely spaced
with Chloroquine, deranged by the orange cocktails

the barstaff of the Shangri La had named for us
and now will mix no more, I dreamt you'd pawned
your children for the last one in the class –

unchampioned by Braxton, Kirk or Zorn,
the articulate gold-lacquered stick insect
of some three-inch-long B*b* hyperhorn

that five tunes in, you nonchalantly plucked
from your shirt, and took a long and silent solo
(on the changes of *Countdown*, I somehow clocked)

as every bat in Kota Kinabalu
flew headlong into the nearest tree,
and all the street-dogs went completely lulu

while the audience bled appreciatively
from their ears. But no, our real exit
was the usual trip; exotic ignominy.

What do we have to show for all our sweat,
beside the flight-case, dense with the scars
and badges of our campaigns? Not a note:

the good ones I was way too gone to hear;
the bad I forget. What work is so defeated
by itself, as all our scribbling in the air?

All I have is this: you, undisputed
king of static, stung by lift and door
and carpet, finally electrocuted

by a cappuccino in a Polish bar;
the pale girl in Szeged, who blanked me, two
years later, in Szeged; the joyous roar

as we touched down on a groove cut from the snow
in a Trebzon whiteout; the drunk who kicked my stand
halfway across the stage in Visingsö;

our hellhole digs in Goole, the night the barman
solemnly engraved a perfect arse
in my Guinness; and one small hour on the M1

with Christine in the back seat of the car
giving it *Spring Can Really Hang You Up*
two inches, then one inch from my right ear

so long and low and sad and slow and hip
I was paralysed down one side
till Watford Gap.

In half an hour we'll either both be dead
or standing at the old black carousel
awaiting the traditionally delayed

arrival of your ton-weight king-size jonquil
plastic suitcase. I won't miss it for a while
but I'll lift it for you man, this once, the hell.

The Shut-in

Good of them, all told, to leave me locked
inside my favourite hour: the whole one early
I came to wait for one I loved too dearly
in this coffered snug below the viaduct
with my dark vernacular ale, Stevenson's
short fiction, and the little game I played
of not thinking of her, except to thumb away
the exquisite stitch that gathers at my breastbone.

The minute hand strains at its lengthening tether
like Achilles on the hare; the luscious beer
refills; the millionth page flowers on the last
of *The Bottle Imp* . . . O Fathers, leave me here,
beyond the night, the stars, beyond the vast
infinitesimal letdown of each other!

Web

The deftest leave no trace: type, send, delete,
clear *history*. The world will never know.
Though a man might wonder, as he crossed the street
what it was that broke across his brow
or vanished on his tongue and left it sweet

Three Poems after Cavafy

One Night

The room above the bar
was the cheapest we could find.
We could see the filthy alley
from the window, hear the shouts
of the workmen at their card-games.

Yet there on that narrow bed
I had love's body, knew its red lips;
those lips so full, so bloody with desire
that now as I write, after so many years,
in this lonely house . . . I'm drunk with them again.

The Boat

This little pencil sketch –
it's certainly him.
It was made quickly, one long
charmed afternoon
on the Ionian. Yes, I'd say
it caught his looks –
though I have him more handsome;
so much the sensualist, you'd say
he was lit up with it . . . Yes, he looks
so much more handsome,
now my heart calls him
from so long ago. So long.
All these things are very old – the sketch,
and the boat, and the afternoon.

The Bandaged Shoulder

He said he'd hurt himself on a wall, or had fallen,
but no doubt there was some other reason
for the wound, for the bandaged shoulder.

He was reaching up to the shelf for a photograph
he wanted to look at more closely
when the bandage came undone. A little blood ran.

I did it up for him again, taking far too much time
over the binding; he wasn't in pain,
and – to be honest – I liked looking at the blood.
That blood. It was all part of my love.

When he left, I found a strip torn from the bandage
under his chair, a rag I should have thrown
straight in the trash – but I picked up and raised it to my lips,
and kept there a long while:
his blood on my lips, O my love, my love's blood.

My Love

It's not the lover that we love, but love
itself, love as in nothing, as in O;
love is the lover's coin, a coin of no country,
hence: the ring; hence: the moon –
no wonder that empty circle so often figures
in our intimate dark, our skin-trade,
that commerce so furious we often think
love's something we share; but we're always wrong.

When our lover mercifully departs
and lets us get back to the business of love again,
either we'll slip it inside us like the host
or we'll beat its gibbous drum that the whole world
might know who has it. Which was always more *my* style:

O the moon's a bodhran, a skin gong
torn from the hide of Capricorn,
and many's the time I'd lift it from its high peg,
grip it to my side, tight as a gun,
and whip the life out of it, just for the joy
of that huge heart under my ribs again.
A thousand blows I showered like meteors
down on that sweet-spot over Mare Imbrium
where I could make it sing its name, over and over.
While I have the moon, I cried, *no ship will sink,*
or woman bleed, or man lose his mind –
but truth told, I was terrible:
the idiot at the session spoiling it,
as they say, for everyone.
O *kings* petitioned me to pack it in.

The last time, I peeled off my shirt
and found a coffee bruise that ran from hip to wrist.
Two years passed before a soul could touch me.

Even in its lowest coin, it kills us to keep love,
kills us to give it away. All of which
brings us to Camille Flammarion,
signing the flyleaf of his *Terres du Ciel*
for a girl down from the sanatorium,
and his remark – the one he couldn't *help* but make –
on the gorgeous candid pallor of her shoulders;
then two years later, unwrapping the same book
reinscribed in her clear hand, *with my love,*
and bound in her own lunar vellum.

A Gift

That night she called his name, not mine
  and could not call it back
I shamed myself, and thought of that blind
  girl in Kodiak

who sat out on the stoop each night
  to watch the daylight fade
and lift her child down to the gate cut
  in the palisade

and what old caution love resigned
  when through that misty stare
she passed the boy to not her bearskinned
  husband but the bear

The Wreck

But what lovers we were, what lovers,
even when it was all over –

the deadweight, bull-black wines we swung
towards each other rang and rang

like bells of blood, our own great hearts.
We slung the drunk boat out of port

and watched our unreal sober life
unmoor, a continent of grief;

the candlelight strange on our faces
like the tiny silent blazes

and coruscations of its wars.
We blew them out and took the stairs

into the night for the night's work,
stripped off in the timbered dark,

gently hooked each other on
like aqualungs, and thundered down

to mine our lovely secret wreck.
We surfaced later, breathless, back

to back, then made our way alone
up the mined beach of the dawn.

The Alexandrian Library

Part III: The Book at Bedtime

The bed sees us add ourselves to the world, then subtract ourselves from it;
perhaps that explains its talent for mathematical subversion. A man alone
in bed so often feels half a human, a man and a woman, one – or two plus
a gap so inspissated it becomes a third. And though its white book opens
innocently enough each night, within an hour the sheets have multiplied
a thousand faces, known and unknown. Yet the bed remains our kindest
friend, breaking our first fall, providing our love with its intimate theatre,
dissolving our grief in sleep – and finally lowering us under, with all the
gentleness it can muster, the gentleness of nothing.

François Aussemain, Cahiers

i *The Fall Asleep*

You don't know it quite yet, but this whistling noise
is your call-up, your wheedling come-hither,
the wind in your inchoate lugs as you fall
to that ultimate brand of post-coital triste
known as life. When exactly you kissed the big book
is a mystery to you, but kiss it you did,
and at least now you'll know where the nightmares came from:
the one where you're lured from that high, high-walled garden
by the man at the gatepost, who bends down to ruffle
your hair and to hand you the horror –
a grey caustic putty that turns out to be
the collapsed star of boredom itself
with its instant effect of reversing one-half
of the ten million magnets you had no idea
were making you up. Hence your waking for good
from the dream of the garden to this:

the blur in the bassinet, trying to shake out
ten thousand faces from one little face,
this being the orgy of selves in the hell
of their irresolution – until, with that first
and that only true effort of will
you cram them all into your little white suit,
your good suit, poor wee lamb, your only suit.

ii *Eleventh Hour*

What this is not is that purblind homecoming,
that pulsing upstream to the currentless matrix
unless, since the last time you thrashed your way up here
Exxon or RTZ bought out the lease
and have filled the whole river with rancid molasses.
This, by even your generous benchmarks
goes down as a horrible fuck.
On the bright side, you seem to have failed to attend
to her features sufficiently well to permit you
to dredge up her face from the mortal dark someone –
you can't be sure who – had insisted upon:
wisely, in view of her whisky-breath, chest hair,
bald spot and fairly luxuriant beard.
Heigh ho. She whispers some growly and baritone
nothing, and mercy! you spawn and expire
and are sinking away to some half-tuned dream-channel
when your hand or her hand flies out to the lamp
and you find yourself buried right up your own arse
to the barcode. The look on your face, you presume,
is also precisely the look on your face

and priceless, or would be on anyone else's.
You lie there all night or forever, with both of you
caught in the wild feedback-loop of your screaming
as what you had fancifully fancied your one
unassailable notion, like: *one,* is returned to you
feminised, travestied, whittled away
by unspeakable steady degrees.

iii *Stroke of Midnight*

So much for those short-trousered fantasies – thumbing
her knickers down, taking the head off the goldfish
or eating four packets of Jaffa Cakes.
The last soft thing left in the planet of glass
you tap the cold screens of her eyes with your nail;
her hair is strung hard as a harp, and attempting
to lift her away from your armpit, you find
she comes up in one piece, like a fossil.
You make for the bog, but then wisely decide
that essaying a moonlit, lugubrious slash
à la what-his-puss might not be such a great move,
given it could take a Gödel or Fermier
to work out the spatiotemporal consequence
of that act, and several others. Like crying.
By the tilt of the water inside the U-bend
you infer that the wind must be up.

You rake in the drawer for a torch; things now drag
when you move them, and thereafter suffer
a dreadful nostalgia for where they last lay

till they ache in your hand like a sprain or an isotope.
Outside, the back green is a carpet of tintacks
such is the absolute disinclination
of every grass-blade to be bent one iota.
You edge past a big cuff of wind: it offers
some give, so you shove yourself through it
and on through a series of parallel buffets
like a talentless ghost through the walls of a castle
till you reach it: the sundial. Your watch being useless,
you will check on the time with your torch.
You stand for a month or so, till on a bored whim
you slash up your wrist on a moth, and a handful
of garnets go rattling onto the lawn.
You head back to bed, lift up the quilt
as you might the top half of a gigantic clam,
slump into your socket, replace your hard friend
miserably under your armpit again
and then wait in the soundless dark, for a sound.

iv *Small Hour*

A noise. You are shouting, but nowhere as loud
as you think you are. She stirs in the dark.
You are where are you? Oh aye. You're here again,
bunking off Beatrice's launch down at Zeppo's,
holed up with your mobile switched off in some wee town
like Alyth or Methil to ham up your accent
and pursue, as you do once a year, what your female friends
nastily caricature as *The Dream*
of the Spiritually Realised but Analphabetic

Nymphet. Her slim shoulder fits into your oxter
like a dovetailjoint, and she will sleep for a while yet.
While you're charmed to your socks by her proud ignorance
of who Socrates was, what meteorites are,
what you do for a living and whereabouts Panama
is on the map, you know that this feeling
is somehow all wrong; though derive no small comfort
reminding yourself that despite all their knee-jerk
and modish disdain, none of the posse'd
be seen dead round here in the first place –
being all bitter-ending at Beatrice's launch
having hoovered the last of the blinis, prosecco
and toot off the top of the cistern.

Your life has a smack of the prequel about it –
a bit underfunded, with you just a trifle
miscast in the role of the younger yourself.
Despite your impressive portfolio of shortcomings
you are not a bad lad, you have come to accept,
on balance, more blessing than blight; though if pressed
you could give the addresses of ten or twelve folk
inclined to feel otherwise, deeply.
Some call you an angel. Some call you a cunt.
They are both on the money: you model yourself
on those various itinerant Johnnies, proclaiming
the Matraiya, the Christ, in the meantime attaining
a kind of provisional, rough-hewn beatitude
before He shows up and comes down on your shagging
and drinking and lapses in personal hygiene.
At which point it's offski: *what need do I have*

for that or for this? I dance at the feet
of my Lord; all is bliss, all is bliss.
Here is my head on a plate and my arse
in a sling, for I'm done with them both, O my Saviour.

Deep down, though, you know you'll do all this again;
your unspeakable habits have laid such deep ruts
in the pit of that mile-deep arroyo your numberless
past lives have worn in the carvable ether
of fate, it is only a matter of time
till some runaway soul-train* will hit them again.

You can see it all now: the bed made with you in it,
the horseshoe of lovely stepdaughters; the locker
of sun-cracked formica, the jug of stale water,
the white poke of fused barley sugar and *Middlemarch*
still lying triumphantly closed; then the light
and the throb as you plough your way under.
You manage to tick off the first thirteen stations
but then you go missing the Ground Luminescence
as usual, still blaming the morphine, whoever
translated the *Bardo Thötröl* in the Penguin
and the time when Miss Houston exploded two fingers

*(I say 'soul', but dear children – I mean mine, reader, mine –
it is not the soul that's reborn, we have none –
but the character, being precisely the shape
of our earthly desire. Read these lines when I'm dead
and know this: despite all I could do to prevent me
I am walking amongst you again.)

54

of chalk with her tawse on your very first day
in Primary One. As a warning.
Since then you took bad with surprises.

Then it's the old routine: running the infinite
gauntlet of demons all wearing your face
before plumping again with pathetic relief
for the baby-blue light that is Orbis Humanis
seen from up here, from where you are.

After your ninemonth *in utero* rehab
you'll hit the ground running as usual, and make
the worst of all possible starts:
penetrating a woman – your mum, of all folk –
with completely unreasonable force.
You would have you arrested. This violence is due,
you will wryly observe (remembering your Dawkins,
before all the books of your last life flare up
in the blistering light of the new) to the size
of your brain; an attribute you and your mother,
for different reasons, agree is not everything.
Ochone, ochone.

In the meantime there is just this, which will do:
the qualified bliss of your once-more deferred
enlightenment, the plagal and imperfect cadences,
all those blessed suspensions of faith, as you lie
in the strong and small arms of your good and kind sister
with nothing much better or worse to look forward to
than your coffee, the paper, the dog on the bed.

v *Dawn: Neverland*

Daylight: you scrabbling up through the exorcised,
grassed-over malebolge of Kirrie Den,
emerging nose-first from the turndown
into this, the big book of my little life.
Through a panel of secondary glazing in Thrums
the pale Angus dawn pours slowly like honey
over the billion wee interlocked hexagons
on Annie's right shoulder. This, for the record
is where, son, we are with it now.

Chez Barrie, up on the Brechin Road,
the presence of Tinkerbell, crappily signified
by a lightbulb revolving round four bits of mirror
will not make itself felt for some hours yet.
Annie is stirring, and mutters a curse
in Nepali directed at whoever's stealing
her big plate of buffalo yoghurt. Behind three doors
Alice Rhianna and Ester are breathing
slow slower and slowest; downstairs
the hamster puts in his last hour at the wheel
and the twins are still sleeping, since this is a poem.
Long shadows yawn between the wee school
and the field set aside for the Peter Pan Complex.
Maybe they'll have free admission for sufferers
Annie said last night, this reinforced
by a stare at the back of your head. Sorry. Mine.

I grew away eight miles due south of the Sidlaws
and grow home eight miles to the north of them,
their image reversed in the back bedroom window
like some slow beast turned round in its cage.
Here is my geomythology, friend:
nine maidens there were in the Howe of Strathmartine
who were all swallowed whole by a dragon.
A pub on the scheme bears their name, while my old school
took that of the beast. Cross over the Fairyhills
and, blow me down, we find nine maidens also
in Charleston-by-Glamis, all of whom became saints.
I like this side better, free from the serpent
if with some overemphasis placed on the virtues
of service and work. In my rimy red shed
the timer-switch clicks on the heating.
I dream of the Gairie, its ancient autochthonous
seam, and I set myself down like a paper boat
till the mind is a little white flag in the current
sailing under the tunnel, back into the Den,
past the stone train which the council removed,
past the green banks stung with hawkbit and celandine
to alight at the bridge and walk over to pay
the blind man at the booth for a ball and a stick
and then onto the green I read O! like a book,
and waft the white featherpack over the swale
where you wait with the pin and pull at its approach
and the whole place starts ticking. The crocodile swaggers
up from the burn and

No No. I have merely
fallen asleep in my watch. Five more
then it's up, then it's *out of yer pit, Donald* –

as my old dear would say, my mother, my ma,
who lives a few miles down the road from here. Five more
to pull it together again, you and I,
and raise the beast up to the sun.

Twinflooer

(Linnaea Borealis)

Tho' it grows
in oor baald east
alane, it's still
sic an antrin baste
I anely find it
in dwam or dream,
an catch them
in thir lemanrie
hunkered alow
a wheesh't circle
cut clean fae
the blackie-sang
or lintie-sang
as ower a cairn,
or wirrikow
in a field o corn.
I pert the girss
an' there they are,
the shilpit pair
cried for him
wha rived a kingdom
in twa estates –
an' gently lift
the pallie, lither
bells thegither:
twa fingertips
tak'in up
the exact wecht
o nothin, licht

as the twa-fauld name
on yer ane jimp stem.

Win'-balance,
elf-cleek,
breist o silence –
a word hauf-swicked
fae the fa' o Babel,
whitever it spelt
sae slicht and nesh
it jinked the trouble,
and rode the jaw
as the broch tummel't
t' somehow waash
up here, a trick
or holy geg
like the *twa-in-yin*
breathed in the lug
o the blin'fauld halflin.

Lass, they say
oor nation's nae
words for *love*
the wiy we have
for daith, or deil.
Times ye feel
the mair wi gang
intil thon tongue –
hidden, fey
an' ayebydan –

the less wi hae
the need o ane.
And jist the same,
there's nae flooer here
aside the yin
I've here descreivit;
yet merk this pair,
strecht fae Ovid,
nailed thegither
wame to wame –
tynt in the ither,
ayont a' thocht,
a' deed, a' talk,
hauf-jyned, hauf-rift:
thir heids doverin
unner the licht
         yock
o the lift

baald – bald; *antrin* – rare, singular; *baste* – beast; *dwam* –
daydream; *lemanrie* – sexual or illicit love; *wheesh't* – stilled; *blackie* –
blackbird; *lintie* – linnet; *cairn* – burial mound; *wirrikow* –
scarecrow, demon; *girss* – grass; *shilpit* – thin, weak; *cried* – called;
rived – split; *pallie* – pale; *lither* – lazy; *wecht* – weight; *licht* – light;
twa-fauld – two-fold; *jimp* – slender; *win'* – wind; *cleek* – hook;
swicked – cheated; *slicht* – slight; *nesh* – soft; *jinked* – dodged; *jaw* –
wave, breaker; *broch* – tower; *geg* – gag, joke; *twa-in-yin* –
supposedly 'the horseman's word'; *blin'fauld* – blindfolded; *halflin* –
adolescent; *daith* – death; *deil* – devil; *gang* – go; *fey* – doomed;
ayebydan – eternal; *descreivit* – described; *strecht* – straight; *wame* –
belly; *tynt* – lost; *ayont* – beyond; *thocht* – thought; *doverin* –
nodding in sleep; *yock* – yoke; *lift* – sky, heavens

Palm

after Rilke

Nowadays, this footsole treads on nothing
but air and nerve; sometimes it hails itself
in its own rippled glass, and in such attitude
knows it holds the map of heaven's streets,
being a thousand rivers, all with one name.
A small christ, it will walk across a stream,
weigh up the rain, or rest on the black mirror
of a well; it steps brightly into other hands
and turns those that it loves into new heavens,
rivers it revives, replenishes,
flooding them with arrival and arrival.

Archaic Torso of Apollo

after Rilke

You'll never know that terrific head,
or feel those eyeballs ripen on you –
yet something here keeps you in view,
as if his look had sunk inside

and still blazed on. Or the double axe
of the breast couldn't blind you, nor that grin
flash along the crease of the loins
down to the low centre of his sex.

Or else he'd sit, headless and halved,
his shoulders falling to thin air –
not shiver like the pelt of a wolf

or burst from his angles like a star:
for there is nowhere to hide, nothing here
that does not see you. *Now change your life.*

The Long Story

i.m. Rev. Francis Cougan, 1907–95

"Well, to cut a long story short," *said old Frank,*
  who lay dying in his room off the ward
"they were all running down to the shore with their nets,
  chasing the funny wee bird –

when two children walked out from under the dune.
  They both had black eyes and black hair
and black bathing suits – even little black spades.
  They didn't speak. No: they just stared.

Claire piped up first. 'Who are you, then?' she asked.
  'She's Pansy,' said Paddy. 'He's Paddy,'
said Pansy – but both at once, so it was lucky
  that Claire knew the story already.

'Can you help us?' said Paddy. 'We've found something strange.
  It's heavy and square and it . . . talks.'
And sure enough, under the dune was a hole,
  and inside the hole was a box.

'Wow! Maybe it's treasure!' said Catherine. 'Or money!'
  said Stephen. 'Or custard!' said Claire.
'Or empty,' said Donald. 'But now the bird's gone –
  we might as well find out what's there.'

Well they peched and they panted for over an hour,
  and to cut a long story . . . well, short –
when they'd lifted the box out, they heard a wee voice,
  and the voice sounded very distraught.

64

'Let me out! Let me out! Will you *please* let me out!'
    Stephen took out his knife. 'Stop!
Suppose it's an imp?' shouted Claire – but he shrugged,
    and levered the lid off the top.

'Yeuch! That's *disgusting!*' said Donald. No wonder –
    it was truly a sight to behold,
like the turkey leftovers at Christmas, but covered
    with feathers and treacle and mould.

'Thanks!' said the feathery mess. Then a finger
    stuck out; it was yellow and thin.
'Look – could you please go and get some sea-water,
    and pour it back into the tin?'

So they all went and dipped their six pails in the waves
    and then filled up the box with the brine.
In a great hiss of steam, something crawled from the box
    like washing wound out on a line.

Its face was as white as the moon and its wings
    were as big as the bridge on the Forth.
Stephen spoke first. 'You're a . . .' 'What?' said the angel.
    'Oh . . . aye. Always have been. Since birth.'

'So how long've you been there?' asked Donald. 'And how did . . .'
    'Oh – centuries. And it's a long . . .
well maybe some other time. Now: make a wish.
    Just the one, now, so don't get it wrong.'

Now Catherine remembered she'd read in a book
        that the wishes of angels were not
quite the same as those doled out by genies or elves
        where whatever you asked for, you got.

With angels it all went the other way round
        and you get the reverse of your wish.
If you ask for a kite it'll give you a brick.
        If you ask for a parrot, a fish.

'I . . . want nothing at all,' she said. 'What?' muttered Claire
        which got her a kick in the shins.
'I mean . . . aye! Me too – nothing!' 'Yup – nothing for me,'
        said Donald, not very convinced.

'Well . . . I'll have a year off the school and a bike
        and some money and sweeties as well –'
said Stephen, or probably would have if Claire
        hadn't covered his head with her pail.

'What was that?' said the angel. 'Och . . . nothing,' said Catherine.
        'Him too then. Good – nothing all round!'
Stephen scowled as he took off the bucket, but knew
        from their faces he daren't make a sound.

'Close your eyes, and wish hard, then.' And that's what they did,
        though wishing for nothing is hard.
When they looked again – guess what? The angel and Paddy
        and Pansy had all disappeared,

but stranger than that – just one person called Catherine-
     andDonaldandStephenandClaire
stared with one big eye, and all that they saw
     in the earth, sea and sky was all theirs.

And, as they stood there amazed at their luck
     they heard a clip-clop and a whinny
and who should ride up with his cuddy and trap
     but – you guessed! It was Caravan Johnny.

He stood with his back to the gigantic sun
     (by then it was getting quite late)
and it looked for the world like his shaggy old head
     had been stuck on a big golden plate.

'Where've you been all day?' Stephen asked Johnny.
     'I had to gang oot for a chat
with a wee man in Otherland,' Johnny replied.
     'Oh,' said Claire. 'Why's it called that?'

'Well, the rivers and flooers are all cried efter ships
     and the birds and the clouds efter trees,
and the stars efter fish – they use oor words for things,
     but well . . . swap them aroond as they please.'

'So everything's – called something else, then?' asked Catherine.
     'They jist hae the yin great big word
that does for maist a'thin. It's a la . . . onyway:
     I've been sent back to find a wee bird –

it's escaped to this world – and I'd best get it hame
    afore the king kens it's gone missin'.
It's his favourite.' 'So . . . how can you spot it?' asked Stephen,
    and they all leant in closer to listen.

'Well . . . its voice is ower high to be heard, and it flies
    almost too fast for oor sicht to follow –
though if it sits doon, ye can't see it at aa'.
    It's quite like a swift or a swallow,

though its een are bricht blue and its feathers as white
    as a swan's, only ten times as brilliant – '"
But Scheherazade saw the approach of the dawn
    and discreetly fell silent

'96

her sleek
thigh
on my
cheek

a flayed
tongue
in the wrong
head

no poem
all year
but its dumb

inverse
sow's ear
silk purse

Colophon

F— , d'ye remember that dolphin, after the pine marten and the Sika fawn, the last on our ticklist of the local fauna? We'd watched it rest all morning on the west side of the loch; it had barely moved in an hour. It was the day after Stephen had gone, the day after the storm; the power had been knocked out again, this time, it seemed, for good. Whether it was the stink of paraffin and dead candles, or my five-day booze and caffeine diet, or just the fact I was on holiday, I had a headache like thunder; come half two, I took three Nurofen and hit the sack.

– Praying, as usual, that you'd follow me through; that beautiful pause; and you always would, and did, letting me stiffen under your cool hand till, before we knew it, it became a hitch, a copla, a hyphen between us, something as much yours as mine, or neither, no part of us, till we were both lost on the bridge of it. Twenty minutes later, though, I was locked in my old dependable Calvinist *tristesse*. I should've bought that stage-coffin at the boot sale when you suggested it, so I could just roll into it afterwards, close the lid and sleep it off.

Anyway, I sank into that favourite dream where I somehow get my thumbnail under the skin of the loch, and strip it off like cellophane, then wrap myself in it, head to foot: it's a kind of icy chiffon, this impossibly fine stuff of cold skies and thin sunrises, stitched with the blurred motifs of gannet and puffin . . . And I'm walking out onto the shore with this hooded sky-coat, my mirror-coat, till I'm stood before that horrible phoney conifer we saw once, a cloak of ivy hung on the bones of a dead elm . . . And because it wouldn't reflect in the flayed loch – none of the trees would now, *mea culpa* – it gave out this dreadful pained roar, a noise like nails thrown in a wood-shredder, and I woke myself with one shout.

Stillness. The tap next door like a tiny xylophone. You'd gone, I guessed, to call your father, the phonebox a halfhour walk down Loch Fyne. I got up and headed out – light, voided, even; the sun was gone and the moon high, trailing in its path like an orphan. For the life of me I couldn't find it anywhere in the water.

I went down to the lochside to empty some more of the beach, wishing I was eight again, back on that slate quarry in Easdale with my father, that glassy oval lochan, and every stone we lifted the fit and weight of a sleek fobwatch; we made them patter out into infinity all afternoon . . . It was *too* perfect: we were daft with it, and something seemed to deafen us – I remember my mother calling on us . . . and our returned silence as a pact, almost a formal response, an antiphon. Today, though, nothing would skip more than once or twice.

What do you call the opposite of epiphany? How'd you define that particular dereliction, that feeling that you said you got as a child when you'd wail and greet and plead and finally got hold of the other bairn's toy, and realised that was no fun either? And worse, that the problem was you?

I didn't tell you this. Further down the shore I saw him again, and sat down at the brimming edge, waiting for him to come to me . . . *come over, come over* – ecstatic, for a few seconds, O I was Arion rescued, then suddenly I knew what I was looking at: the dead cormorant, stopped in mid-crawl, the stiff fan of its wing raised like a black sail, damn it, damn it, like a perfect fin.

The Sea at Brighton

To move through your half-million furnished hours
as that gull sails through the derelict tearooms
of the West Pier; to know their shadowed realm
as a blink, a second's darkening of the course . . .

The bird heads for the Palace, then skites over
its blank flags, whitewashed domes and campaniles,
vanishes. Today, the shies and stalls
are locked, the gypsies off to bank the silver;

the ghosts have left the ghost train, and are gone
from every pebble, beach-hut, dog and kite
in the blanket absolution of the light
of a November forenoon. It is that long

instant, when all the vacant forms
are cast upon the ground, that hinge in the day
when the world and its black facsimile
lie open like the book of perfect names.

Old stone-grinder, sky-face, pachyderm,
I render them to you. Now let me walk along
those empty roads above your listening.
I write this on the first morning of term

back home from the country of no songs,
between the blue swell and the stony silence
right down where the one thing meets the millions
at the line of speech, the white assuaging tongues.

The Light

When I reached his bed he was already blind.
Thirteen years had gone, and yet my mind
was as dark as on my ordination day.
Now I was shameless. I begged him for the light.
'Is it not taught *all* is illusory?
And still you did not guess the truth of it?
There is no light, fool. Now have you awoken?'
And he laughed, and then he left us. I was broken.

I went back to my room to pack my things,
my begging-bowl, my robe and cup; the prayer-mat
I would leave. It lay there, frayed and framed
in a square of late sun. And out of pure habit –
no, less, out of nothing, for I was nothing –
I watched myself sit down for one last time.

The Black Box

In the fairytales of musicians, you are led to it
by the usual talking dog or sloe-eyed twins
who ask your help to dig it from the dune
or the leafmould. Now – in a normal story –
a faint voice snivels *if you let me out . . .*
then rehearses its extravagant parole;
but here a solid silence is observed,
and when you've carved the block from the wet sand
or prised it from its fist of alder-roots
to work your knife below the lid, you find
another box, then another, and another,
and in the last, a beautiful mute bird.

I refer, of course, to that collapsible
ziggurat, that chocolate-box of darks
known as the Reverberation Unit:
a black box in a glass booth full of dials,
racked up with the EQs and compressors
where it waits to shout back from its seven-inch vault.

But let's hear, in our discourse, no ignorant talk
of 'echo chambers', or of how the truth
can only reach us from the horse's mouth:
that poet's fetish! Remember how it sent
poor Louis marching underground, when all
he needed for those ticking stalactites
was a box of thumbtacks, gently shaken out
in a BBC firebucket, the result
then filtered through the educated drainpipe
of The Great British Spring. Now that immortal coil

has gone the way of all its noble forebears
(from the Watkins Copycat and metal plate
to standing very far away and shouting)
the finest, by unanimous consent,
is the Lexicon, for what we might describe
as its actorly qualities: the human warmth
of its digitised distortions, its vast range
and total lack of personality.

Hence its totem-status in the dreams
of musicians: our reverb falls to earth,
becomes a thing, and then one small enough
to be possessed, and so to be desired.
One tiny anecdote. Late Seventies:
in a spat of clear-air turb three miles above
the spidery Urals, Miroslav Vitous
bends to the next seat, and ashenly
adjusts the belt around his new Space Echo,
all trippy pinks and giant solderboards;
meanwhile in the hold, his double bass
cracks, unseams and opens like a clam.

Now since we're here, we might just take a look
at its unicameral, deaf-mute 2-D sister.
In the nightmares of pilots, you are led to it
by the usual talking wolf or limping child
who asks your help, etcetera, except
a queer tune seems to rise up from the ground –
something the balloon man used to sing,
or that uncle who just visited the once –

and when you work your knife under the lid
the box is just one box, and the bird dead.
Then, behind your back, the song resumes.
Anyway: a black box in a glass booth
full of dials, but for the sake of brevity
let's wind on to its bubbleless descent
through the awful broth of legs and heads
and handluggage and little plastic trays,
down through shoals that part to let it pass
the way a whispering crowd does for a doctor
to the seabed and its calm four-second blip,
the last stats and the co-pilot's *oh shit*
locked inside its thin gut like a pearl.

We might think of our box as its inverse –
a departuary, or antiterminus,
and better understand its high romance
if we state the case in its extreme:
this is the means by which we can extend
our voices to the stars. (A less good trick
than it might sound. Having always dug
far better than we build, all long delays
sounds to us like mineshafts, and not towers –
or, at best, an endless corridor stitched
with one repeated shout, one madman running,
when, as the old two-mirror trick confirms,
it's the corridor we really want to hear
and not ourselves in infinite regress.)

So what we have, then, is an interface
between this room and every other possible
through which we can elect to send a signal –
a voice, a cello or a saxophone –
down this or that divaricating path
of echo and refraction and destruction
to whatever place they whistle up between them.
I say 'send' and 'to', but better to imagine
a laser clicked on in its bagatelle
of prisms and angled mirrors, and then finding
not the half-expected ricochet
of the light-bolt, but its blazing diagram,
held up in the air like a cat's cradle.

So it is here: the ear hallucinates
to relocate the cello or the voice
in an empty auditorium, or the same
full, or two-thirds full, or draped in velvet,
the floor, oakwood or deeply carpeted;
one touch of the dial, and suddenly we're standing
at the foot of the stairs, the top, the cluttered halfpace;
in snowfall or invisible serein,
beech- or pine-woods, galilees or attics,
vast eyesores no man would build, except
to be a strange cathedral for one song;
or in those rooms we're always locked outside –
the mountain, matchbox or the needle's eye –
but can still thread with the disembodied voice.

(Though there are hymns to cancellation too:
I remember sitting in a wooden cell
so deviously hatched and honeycombed
the words were gone an inch before my lips.
It was the hall of mirrors in reverse
and I felt, if such a thing were possible,
that I was fewer.
                            An engineer once told me
that his life was shadowed, every hour of it,
by this specific threat: that should his mind
be read the way the mirror reads your face
and his interlocutor somehow repeat
his words to him one half-a-wavelength out,
they'd disappear completely. Which explains
the silence that we keep in early love,
knowing that to speak would be to hazard
one stolen look in love's own magic glass
and see it emptied of ourselves for good.)

There is a second dial, which regulates
the mix of here-and-now to there-and-then,
the degree to which our designated elsewhere
bleeds into the dry fact of the present
where the present is a dead room with a mike.

Okay; let's pull the plug on it and see
what we have. It is less a locked Versailles
than our proverbial wood, in that split-second
when no one in the universe invokes it.
Here no tree falls, unseen or otherwise,

the constipated bears are all asleep
and the last breath of the cyclone has just failed
to lift the pale wings of the butterfly.
The day is Latter Lammas, Nevermass.
The leaves here fall like anvils and pianos
and so think better of it, mercifully.
It is the Buddha-mind, so still and empty
it desires or needs no song. Powered back up
it is the mind at rest, its dead blue eyes
as steady and as nervelessly unblinking
as Robert Powell's in Zeffirelli's gospel.
Though we only walk the shoreline of those states,
in our best silences, one true word sometimes
forms itself and rises to our lips,
and we hurry it (like that marvellous fish
we might pull from a dream, its scales already
dulling, and the market miles away)
to the place we seemed to have in mind for it –
the silent chapel waiting our one note
to trigger off its liturgy of echoes.

Though music does no more than reel it off
– as if to post the number of the psalm
was somehow in itself sufficient praise –
our verses have to humanise the code:
flesh out those bleak quadratics of the spirit
in birds, sea-crossings and the names of towns,
in rain, and what she wore that afternoon –
as we have fleshed it in the same, within
this empty room we pilot through the world.

In the world, my mother's house, are many mansions.
Somewhere in each of these, one window stands
forever open on the infinite.
It is flagged by the touch of presence on the birdsong
that tells us it just after the rain,
or less, say just the small and lissom air
of aftermath or theft cooling our face
as we pass it in the street or in the woods
or stop the bike before the little bridge
for no reason we can think of or remember,
or by that place in our accounts of things
when the words escape us.

As now, when we both must take our voice
back to the unique stanza of our friends,
to hear it lengthen as the room falls empty
then falls, one day, for good – to leave the voice
free again, and back on its long course.

The Landing

Long months on the rising path
I found where I'd come in
and knew the word of heat, the breath
of air move on my skin

and saw the complex upper light
divide the middle tread
then to my left, the darker flight
that fell back to the dead

So like the ass between two bales
I stopped in the half-shade
too torn to say in which exile
the shame was better paid

And while I stood to dwell upon
my empty-handed quest
I watched the early morning sun
send down its golden ghost

It paused just on the lowest step
as if upon a hinge
then slowly drew the dark back up
like blood in a syringe

and suddenly I did not care
if I had lived or died
But then my hand fell on the lyre
that hung dead at my side

and with as plain a stroke I knew
I let each gutstring sound
and listened to the notes I drew
go echoing underground

then somewhere in the afternoon
the thrush's quick reply –
and in that instant knew I'd found
my perfect alibi

No singer of the day or night
is lucky as I am
the dark my sounding-board, the light
my auditorium

Zen Sang at Dayligaun

As aw we ken o the sternless derk
is the warld it fa's amang
aw we hae o the burn and birk
is thir broon or siller sang

Each pair o een in lift or yird
micht hae them by anither
tho' the birk chants t' nae baist or bird
nor burn tae human brither

For the lyart sang's no' staneyraw,
thon gowden sang's no' stane
an' there's nae burn or birk at aw
but jist the sang alane

dayligaun – twilight; *sternless* – starless; *derk* – dark; *birk* – birch;
siller – silver; *een* – eyes; *lift* – sky; *yird* – earth; *chants* – sings; *baist*
– beast; *lyart* – grizzled, silvered; *staneyraw* – lichen; *gowden* – golden

The White Lie

I have never opened a book in my life,
made love to a woman, picked up a knife,
taken a drink, caught the first train
or walked beyond the last house in the lane.

Nor could I put a name to my own face.
Everything we know to be the case
draws its signal colour off the sight
till what falls into that intellectual night

we tunnel into this view or another
falls as we have fallen. *Blessed Mother,*
when I stand between the sunlit and the sun
make me glass: and one night I looked down

to find the girl look up at me and through
me with such a radiant wonder, you
could not read it as a compliment
and so seek to return it. In the event

I let us both down, failing to display
more than a halfhearted opacity.
She turned her face from me, and the light stalled
between us like a sheet, a door, a wall.

But consider this: that when we leave the room,
the chair, the bookend or the picture-frame
we had frozen by desire or spent desire
is reconsumed in its estranging fire

such that, if we slipped back by a road
too long asleep to feel our human tread
we would not recognise one thing by name,
but think ourselves in Akhenaten's tomb;

then, as things ourselves, we would have learnt
we are the source, not the conducting element.
Imagine your shadow burning off the page
as the dear world and the dead word disengage –

in our detachment, we would surely offer
such offence to that Love that will suffer
no wholly isolated soul within
its sphere, it would blast straight through our skin

just as the day would flush out the rogue spark
it found still holding to its private dark.
But like our ever-present, all-wise god
incapable of movement or of thought,

no one at one with all the universe
can touch one thing; in such supreme divorce,
what earthly use are we to our lost brother
when we must stay partly lost to find each other?

Only by this – this shrewd obliquity
of speech, the broken word and the white lie,
do we check ourselves, as we might halt the sun
one degree from the meridian

then wedge it by the thickness of the book
that everything might keep the blackedged look
of things, and that there might be time enough
to die in, dark to read by, distance to love.

DON PATERSON was born in Dundee in 1963. He works as a musician and editor, and has written three collections of poems, *Nil Nil* (1993), *God's Gift to Women* (1997) – winner of both the T. S. Eliot Prize and the Geoffrey Faber Memorial Prize – and *The Eyes* (1999). *Landing Light* received the 2003 Whitbread Poetry Award and the T. S. Eliot Prize. Paterson lives in Kirriemuir, Angus.

Landing Light is set in Warnock Pro.
Book design by Wendy Holdman.
Composition by Stanton Publication Services, Inc.
Manufactured by Maple Vail on acid-free paper.